WALES

A CELTIC HERITAGE

Roger Thomas & Huw Thomas

Wales and the Welsh nation take a special pride in their country. A dramatically different scenery of hills and mountains rears up abruptly as soon as you cross the border from England, but Wales is also a singular place in many other ways. Its culture and traditions, history and a strong Celtic heritage mark it as a country with its own distinctive character.

Crannog Cantre, Llangorse Lake, Brecon Beacons.

The spirit of Wales has been shaped by many different forces. It is a mythical land of dragons, druids and bards inspired by the nation's Celtic origins, but also one rooted in the harsh realities of the Industrial Revolution. Wales is both a rural heartland and a 21st-century urban nation, a country with an ancient language and an ambitious, modern view of its role on the contemporary world stage. These contradictions dispel the old clichés of a country full of coalmines. What is truly eye-opening about the Wales of today is its sheer variety and evolving history. Despite its comparatively small size and population – less than 150 miles (240 km) from tip to toe, with around three million inhabitants – Wales has an astonishingly varied cultural landscape.

Life in the distant past is recalled at ancient castles which dot the landscape in their hundreds, while more recent history can be relived at the mines, mills and quarries that reshaped the country in the 19th century. Wales is home to Britain's oldest living language and a literary tradition that stretches from prehistory to the present day. These cultural traditions are expressed not only in the Welsh language, but also in the way that they have shaped a passion, lyricism and indelible 'sense of place' you find everywhere in Wales, in English- and Welsh-speaking communities alike.

Wales is a land of singers and storytellers, where male voice choirs rub shoulders with the latest bands, and festivals where bards performing ancient rites are to be found, held alongside literary and musical gatherings with a worldwide cultural reach and relevance.

Contradictions aside, one thing is for certain: Wales is a place where passion and national pride are the order of the day.

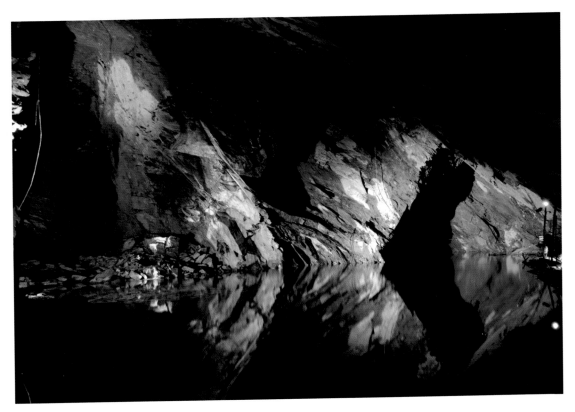

Lake at Llechwedd Slate Caverns.

A CELTIC HERITAGE

You only need look at any road sign in Wales to know you have crossed into a very different country. For non-Welsh speakers, the alternative text below English place names can sometimes seem confusing, but its presence is a constant reminder of Wales's cultural heritage.

Evolving from the Celtic tongue spoken by the ancient Britons, the Welsh language's origins can be traced back to around 500 BC, making it one of the oldest spoken languages in Europe. Some of the earliest-known poems were written in Welsh, and over the centuries the language has proved its resilience by surviving threat from foreign invaders and the spread of linguistic homogeneity.

While English became the official language of Wales during Tudor times, Welsh has always managed to co-exist. The Welsh-language TV channel S4C was launched in 1982, and the latest data shows that over 20 per cent of the population speak Welsh. However that figure is much higher in certain areas. On the Llŷn Peninsula, in Gwynedd, a survey of schools revealed that over 90 per cent of children aged three to 15 were Welsh speakers. The language is at its strongest in the rural north and west, though the resurgence in recent years in people learning and speaking Welsh has been notable in urban areas in the south.

Dewi, a metal dragon sculpture by Tony Peacock, and Harlech Castle beyond.

Wales's literary tradition stretches back many centuries, and is best exemplified by the collection of folk tales contained in the *Mabinogion*. Although they were first written down during the 11th and 12th centuries, the *Mabinogion*'s fantastical tales of dragons,

Right: Ancient Celtic cross in Carew, Pembrokeshire.

A warm welcome greets visitors to Wales.

Welcome to WALES
Croeso i GYMRU

A male voice choir, International Music Eisteddfod, Llangollen.

princes and giants have their origins in a much older tradition of oral storytelling.

In modern times, Wales has been represented by writers such as Dylan Thomas. Although not a Welsh-speaker himself, Thomas incorporated the musicality of the native language into his writing. His masterwork, *Under Milk Wood*, is a 'play for voices' that evokes an indelibly Welsh sense of place and linguistic lyricism.

Music is also a vital component in the cultural heritage of this 'Land of Song'. With their roots in the Nonconformist chapels of the 1800s, the male voice choirs which characterize the close-knit spirit of Welsh communities spread quickly to the collieries and steelworks. Men would gather in industrial villages and towns across the country to sing rousing hymns in one collective voice whose sweet, soaring harmonies contained so much emotion – and said so much about the culture of the time. Nonetheless, many of the choirs founded in the 19th century have proved extraordinarily resilient; the Treorchy Male Voice Choir from the Rhondda Valleys, for example, can trace its history back 125 years and is still going – and singing – strong.

While the choral tradition is alive and well, the musical landscape of Wales has moved on. A line

can be traced right through to the present day, from performers like Tom Jones, Shirley Bassey, Bryn Terfel and Katherine Jenkins, to bands like the Manic Street Preachers and Stereophonics, and singers like Cerys Matthews and Duffy. It is true that Welsh people love to sing and have a strong musical affinity. It is also noteworthy that much of Wales's great music has sprung from the working-class communities to achieve massive success, both at home and worldwide.

The poet Dylan Thomas: detail of a bronze statue at Swansea Marina.

The Red Dragon

The Red Dragon (*Y Ddraig Goch*) which proudly adorns the flag of Wales has a long and complex association with the country. Many stories explain how it became the nation's symbol, but its exact origins are lost to history.

One theory is that the dragon was brought to Wales during the Roman occupation (43–85 AD), in the form of the Draco (Dragon) military standards borne by the invading infantry.

The dragon is also mentioned in ancient texts such as the *Mabinogion* and the *Historia Brittonum*, which is closely linked to legends of King Arthur. One early tale tells of a battle between a native red dragon and an invading white dragon that wreaks havoc across the land. Eventually the dragons are trapped and imprisoned at Dinas Emrys in Snowdonia.

The story continues centuries later, when King Vortigern tries to build a fort at the same location, only for the walls to be demolished by an unseen

The Battle of the Red and White Dragons with the King and Merlin looking on.

The Red Dragon, the emblem of Wales, adorns the national flag.

Caernarfon at the investiture of Edward, Prince of Wales in 1911. However, the current design did not become the country's official flag until 1959.

Today, the Red Dragon remains a symbol of battle, but mainly in the sporting sense. The flag provides a colourful backdrop to the nation's sporting endeavours, most notably in confrontations between the Welsh and English rugby teams.

The leek & the daffodil

Myths tell of Welsh soldiers wearing a leek in their caps at the Battle of Heathfield in 633, to distinguish them from their Saxon foes. Although no one is exactly sure how it came to be a symbol of the country, it is now worn to mark St David's Day, 1 March.

The daffodil has only gained popularity as a Welsh symbol since the early 19th century. This is probably explained by the similarity between the Welsh words for the two plants: *cenhinen* (leek) and *cenhinen pedr* (daffodil).

force each night. A boy, Merlin in some versions of the story, tells the king about the dragons. They are released from their prison to resume battle, the red dragon emerging victorious to become the symbol of Wales's native people.

The banner of the dragon was also closely linked to Cadwaladr, King of Gwynedd between 655 and 682. Though very little is truly known about Cadwaladr, he is immortalized in the stories of Geoffrey of Monmouth as the last in a line of legendary British kings.

Following its mythological beginnings, the Red Dragon became a familiar battle standard. It was said to have been raised at the Battle of Crecy in 1346, when Welsh archers were instrumental in defeating the French. Owain Glyndŵr, the last native-born Prince of Wales, displayed the dragon on his battle standard in his uprising against the English crown in 1400. The symbol also found a home across the border in England. Henry Tudor, founder of the Tudor dynasty, flew the Red Dragon of Cadwaladr both to signify his Welsh heritage and to draw support in his battle against Richard III at Bosworth Field. The dragon – with the addition of the Tudors' green and white livery – subsequently became a familiar symbol while they held the throne between 1485 and 1603. During the reign of King Henry VIII, the flag could be seen flying on Royal Navy ships.

More modern times saw the Red Dragon on a green mount adopted as part of the Royal Badge of Wales in 1807, while the symbol was used in

Daffodils herald the spring.

A LAND OF SONG & DANCE

Wales is home to cultural events that include everything from the country's ancient bardic traditions to music festivals featuring the latest bands.

No event better exemplifies the continuous cultural link between Wales's past and its present than the week-long National Eisteddfod, held in August. The event, held at a different location every year, celebrates Welsh culture and language in all its forms.

The eisteddfod's history can be traced back to 1176, when it is said that the first event was held by Lord Rhys at his castle in Cardigan. Poets and musicians from all over the country were invited, the best being rewarded with a seat at Lord Rhys's table. The modern-day festival, incorporating literature, music, dance, theatre, recitation, visual arts, science and technology, regularly attracts more than 160,000 visitors.

Central to the eisteddfod is the Gorsedd of the Bards. Created in 1792, the Gorsedd is a society of poets, writers and musicians responsible for much of the festival's pageantry. Among the many rites carried out by the Gorsedd is the Chairing Ceremony. Echoing the prize offered by Lord Rhys at the first eisteddfod, it commends the poet judged to have written the best poem, in strict metre on a specific subject. With the bards decked out in colourful robes, the ceremony is a unique celebration of the Welsh literary tradition.

The eisteddfod also embraces contemporary culture. A particular highlight is Maes B, which runs alongside the main event. The largest Welsh-language music festival in the world, it showcases new and established bands and artists from across the country.

A ceremonial fanfare opens the National Eisteddfod.

A talented harpist performs at the National Eisteddfod.

Traditional dancing is a competitive business.

Wales is known as the 'Land of Song' for good reason. Another strand of the country's musical traditions can be seen at the Llangollen International Eisteddfod of Music and Dance, also held in August. Staged annually since 1947, the event was conceived to help rebuild international relationships following the Second World War. The festival is still going strong more than six decades later. Every year more than 4,000 performers from all over the world come to the small North Wales town to take part in concerts and competitions.

One highlight is the prestigious Choir of the World contest for the best overall choir at the eisteddfod. Notable previous competitors include Luciano Pavarotti, who was part of the winning choir from Modena in 1955. He returned as a professional 40 years later for a spectacular concert performance.

Pavarotti is just one of the big names who have performed gala concerts at Llangollen. Over the years, the eisteddfod has featured appearances from a who's who of internationally renowned performers, including Yehudi Menuhin, José Carreras, Kiri Te Kanawa and Bryn Terfel.

The Hay Festival is something of an unlikely success story. Dreamt up around a kitchen table in 1987, what started as a small, family-organized literary event has grown into an internationally recognized extravaganza that takes in books, comedy, music, film and science. Memorably described by former US President Bill Clinton as 'The Woodstock of the mind', the festival has expanded rapidly and now runs spin-off events in such far-flung locations as Nairobi, Cartagena and the Maldives.

Despite – or because of – being far away from the urban centres where such an event might be expected to thrive, the Hay Festival has become possibly the most important date on the UK's literary calendar. Its tented village in green fields on the edge of town has an easy-going, engaging atmosphere that attracts some of the biggest names on the international literary, political and academic scenes.

Familiar signage in the 'town of books'.

Regardless of how far the festival spreads, at its heart it is an expression of the place where it sprung into life. The little border town of Hay-on-Wye has long been famous as a literary hotspot. Boasting more than 30 second-hand and antiquarian bookshops, visitors have been flocking to this quirky 'town of books' for many years in search of rare volumes and bargain paperbacks.

FARMING & FESTIVALS

A traditionally Welsh festival experience can be found at the Royal Welsh Agricultural Show, taking place every July at the Llanelwedd Showground on the outskirts of Builth Wells in Mid Wales.

The Royal Welsh is the largest agricultural show in Europe, regularly attracting more than 200,000 visitors over the course of four days. The event draws farming folk from far and wide to compete in various categories. Breeders bring prized specimen cows, horses and pigs in the hope of being crowned Grand Champion. There are also sheepdog trials, sheep-shearing competitions and displays of falconry and rural crafts.

A herdsman and his prize bull, at The Royal Welsh Show, Builth Wells.

Although essentially a farming show, the Royal Welsh attracts a big audience from town as well as country. The Food Hall, selling all kinds of tasty treats, is a big hit with everyone, along with the many stallholders that set up shop here, the entertainment from motorcycle stunt teams and performances by the Regimental Band and Corp of Drums of the Royal Welsh Infantry Regiment.

Welsh Sheep dog trials test the skills of both the farmer and her dog.

Aside from the spectacle, the show is an important social gathering. It is the only time of year when many of Wales's farmers have the chance to get together, catch up on the news and gossip, and enjoy a few days away from the daily chores.

❀ Music on starry nights ❀

For a few days each summer the sleepy market town of Brecon becomes a hotspot for jazz fans. It is a stellar event, attracting some of the biggest names in the world of jazz ('a dazzlingly diverse set of musical distractions'). Then there is the Green Man which, since 2003, has grown from a folk festival attended by just a few hundred people to a music and arts event that welcomes more than 10,000 festival-goers each August to its picturesque site in the Usk Valley.

🌸 Dylan Thomas Festival 🌸

Celebrating the life of Wales's most famous writer, this festival features poetry, literature, art, theatre and music. Taking place every autumn at the Dylan Thomas Centre in Swansea (his 'ugly, lovely' home town) it explores the writer's work and influence, as well as providing a platform for a new generation of Welsh artists.

🌸 St David's Day 🌸

With its roots stretching back to the 6th century, St David's Day takes place on 1 March every year. Many Welsh people wear a leek or daffodil, and children attend school in traditional Welsh dress to commemorate the day in 589 when Wales's patron saint is reputed to have died.

The ceremonial band of The Royal Welsh Regiment, at Cardiff Castle on St David's Day.

St David's Day parade at Wales Millennium Centre, Cardiff.

A LAND OF CASTLES

The fortresses that dot Wales are undoubtedly amongst the country's most iconic features – Wales is, after all, known as a 'Land of Castles'. Amazingly, there are more than 400 of these. Most of the best-known were built in the 13th century by King Edward I as part of his campaign to subdue what he saw as the unruly natives. Despite being the work of foreign invaders, they are now deeply embedded in the Welsh landscape. These and the many other castles, some built by invading armies, others by the native princes of Wales, give visitors a compelling insight into life and strife in Wales's past, both through the historic strongholds themselves and today's re-enactments and events which take place within them.

Conwy Castle's stunning illuminations reinforce its drama.

The story of castle-building really began at **Chepstow**, reputedly the first stone-built fortress to be constructed in Britain. Work started here in 1067 at a strategic spot on the River Wye, just after the Norman Conquest. Over the next several hundred years the castle expanded and evolved, making the current fortress a document in stone of the changing chapters in architectural style. The castle has many outstanding features. The hall-keep, for example, is the earliest known secular stone building in Britain, while the 800-year-old castle doors are the oldest in Europe.

Regular events at Chepstow recreate life at the castle in times gone by. Re-enactments involve everything from medieval archers and hand gunners to 17th-century musketeers and cannoneers. In noisy but thankfully bloodless displays, large groups of combatants recreate the sights and sounds of conflict at different periods during the castle's history.

Chepstow Castle dominates the town and overlooks the River Wye.

Mighty **Caernarfon** Castle, possibly Wales's most famous fortress, was built by King Edward I not just as a stronghold but as a statement, symbol and seat of royal power. Everything about the huge construction is designed with this regal statement in mind. It was designed to echo the imperial power of Rome and, unlike Edward's other castles, has looming towers that are sharply polygonal rather than rounded. The massive Eagle Tower alone is enough to cast an intimidating shadow over the town.

Caernarfon soon became the administrative centre of North Wales. In 1284 it saw the birth of Edward's son, the first English Prince of Wales, further cementing the king's dominance over the native population.

Caernarfon is one of a quartet of castles built by Edward I that have been declared World Heritage Sites. Along the coast is **Conwy**, well-preserved without and within. Perched on a rock above the Conwy Estuary, the castle's eight round towers are as imposing now as they must have been when originally constructed. They came at a price: Conwy was the most expensive of Edward's castles, costing an estimated £15,000 in the currency of the time, a fortune today.

The outer ward contains a great hall, chambers and kitchen, while the inner ward holds private rooms and the royal chapel. A quick climb up to the battlements provides further revelations in the form of a breathtaking vista of the Snowdonia skyline. And no trip to Conwy is complete without a walk along its exceptionally intact medieval walls that encircle the town, built as an extension of the castle.

The polygonal towers of Caernarfon Castle.

❀ Princes of Wales ❀

The title 'Prince of Wales' can be traced back to medieval times, when it was conferred on the most powerful Welsh ruler of the period. Several great Welsh leaders used the title, including Llywellyn ap Gruffudd, Llewellyn the Last.

Edward I crowned his son Edward – born at Caernarfon Castle – as Prince of Wales in 1301. Owain Glyndŵr, the native leader who led an uprising at the start of the 15th century, was the only Welshman to wrest the title back, albeit briefly.

Prince Charles, the current Prince of Wales, was invested at Caernarfon Castle on 1 July 1969.

Set on cliffs not far from the sea, **Harlech** Castle has similarly commanding views. Despite being constructed in just 12 years and being the least expensive castle Edward I built, it has a reputation for impregnability. Some of this is as a result of its position on sheer west-facing cliffs, but much credit must go to the massive, incredibly strong east gatehouse. Complementing its robust physical features, the castle has another secret weapon. A staircase cut into the rock, descending 200 feet (60 metres) to the foot of the cliffs below, allowed Harlech to be resupplied from the sea, giving it a tremendous advantage when under attack from hostile forces.

Harlech's resilience was put to the test most famously during the Wars of the Roses when it withstood a seven-year siege. This is the longest recorded siege in British history and is said to be the inspiration for the song *Men of Harlech*. Notably, this English-built stronghold briefly became the de facto capital of an independent Wales when it was occupied by Owain Glyndŵr, the country's last native prince, between 1404 and 1409.

Harlech Castle, dramatically situated between the sea and mountains.

Beaumaris Castle on the Isle of Anglesey is the last of the World Heritage quartet. It was also the last of the four to be built and, although lacking the lofty grandeur of the others, is widely considered to be the most architecturally accomplished. Bounded by a large moat, the castle's concentric defences are almost geometric in their symmetry

❈ Owain Glyndŵr, ❈ Prince of Wales

The last native Welshman to hold the title of Prince of Wales, Owain Glyndŵr's uprising against English rule in the early 15th century has guaranteed his legendary status.

Born to a noble Anglo-Welsh family, Glyndŵr fought on the English side in a number of conflicts, notably against Scotland in 1394 and 1395. However, a dispute with his neighbour Reginald de Grey at the end of the 14th century escalated into an all-out Welsh rebellion that lasted some 15 years.

Glyndŵr was proclaimed Prince of Wales in 1400, but his dream of an independent Welsh state was eventually quashed.

Built in the 13th century by Gilbert 'the Red' de Clare, a nobleman of Norman descent, the castle combined defensive solidity with comfortable living quarters for its most important inhabitants. Once Edward I had successfully quelled the Welsh threat from Llewellyn, Prince of Gwynedd, the castle ceased to be of significant strategic importance. By the 19th century it had largely fallen into ruin. Luckily, the third Marquess of Bute, also responsible for the restoration of Cardiff Castle, began preservation works that ensured Caerphilly's survival.

Nowadays Caerphilly is a venue for regular events recalling its long history. These include the opportunity to see medieval siege engines in action, watch archery displays, hear medieval music and see craftsmen at work using ancient tools and skills. At Christmas, the castle and town holds a medieval fair, with seasonal food, traditional gifts, music and entertainment.

and would have been virtually impregnable in the days before gunpowder. Despite its supreme capability, Beaumaris was never really tested in Edward's time, only seeing serious action during the Civil War several centuries later.

In South West Wales, **Pembroke** Castle has a grandeur all of its own. It stands on a rocky promontory above Milford Haven, its mighty stone keep rising to nearly 80 feet (24 metres) and unusual barbican defended by three portcullises. Pembroke is the only castle in Britain to be built over a natural cavern, a large cave known as the Wogan. The castle keep was built by the powerful William Marshal, Earl of Pembroke, in the late 12th century, and in 1457 Pembroke was the birthplace of Henry Tudor, who became King Henry VII. Oliver Cromwell himself came to besiege the castle in 1648, during the Civil War.

Caerphilly Castle, in the south-west, is the largest castle in Wales and the second-largest in Britain after Queen Elizabeth II's residence at Windsor. Only recently has this 'slumbering giant' received the recognition it deserves. Encircled by a series of moats and lakes, again on the concentric principle, it remains a formidable powerhouse even today.

Romantic Beaumaris Castle at sunset.

Not every castle in Wales was built by the Norman and English invaders. There are a few true Welsh castles to be found, such as **Dolbadarn** at Llanberis and **Dolwyddelan** near Betws-y-Coed. Both were built by Llewellyn the Great, Prince of Gwynedd, in the 11th century. Though they may lack the grandeur of many of the castles that came after them, they stand proud in the landscape as atmospheric monuments to a time of trouble and strife, completing the picture of Wales's medieval past.

Dolwyddelan Castle amid the mists of Snowdonia.

For sheer drama, few Welsh castles can rival **Carreg Cennen**. Perched on a towering cliff top near Llandeilo, overlooking the brooding Black Mountain, the castle dominates its surroundings as all great castles should, with a sheer rockface on one side and steep hills on the other. The castle as we now see it was built in the 13th century on the site of an earlier Welsh construction, changing hands several times until it was demolished during the Wars of the Roses.

Even in its ruined form, Carreg Cennen has an aura and power which few others can match. Stumpy, weatherbeaten remains command huge views in all directions, while its walls merge almost imperceptibly with the cliffs on which they stand.

Unlike Carreg Cennen, **Cardiff** Castle has demonstrated an impressive ability to move with the times. Originally the site of a Roman fort, it became an important Norman stronghold before being re-imagined as a Gothic fantasy

in the Victorian era. Perched on its motte, the Norman-built stone keep immediately catches the eye, but it is the impact of the Bute family, the castle's final inhabitants, that is the most evident. In the mid-19th century, the fabulously wealthy Marquess of Bute began a project to remodel the castle as a modern-day Camelot, embellishing its interior in a range of exotic styles. A walk through the castle is a dizzying journey through elaborately decorated Arabian, Mediterranean and Italian-inspired chambers.

Bute's love of the fantastical is continued at **Castell Coch** near Cardiff, where fairy tale whimsy stands in sharp contrast to the warlike demeanour of many Welsh castles. One look tells you that it is, in fact, a fake – but an exceedingly enchanting, romantic one. Despite being built on the site of a genuine 13th-century fortification, Castell Coch was never intended as a defensive structure. Instead, it symbolizes a Victorian interest in the more romantic aspects of the Middle Ages.

Constructed in the late 1880s as a rural retreat for the immensely wealthy Marquess of Bute, away from his main residence at Cardiff Castle, Castell Coch takes its inspiration from fantasy rather than reality. While its three conical spires may have been unsuitable from a military perspective, there can be no doubt that they fulfil the aesthetic objective for which they were designed. This is Sleeping Beauty's castle, not a stronghold intended to rule with an iron fist. The castle's interior is every bit as fanciful as its exterior.

No expense was spared on ornate chambers packed with colourful carvings, and other decorative features including monkeys, butterflies and nesting birds.

Castell Coch might lack the authenticity of Wales's more venerable castles, but it remains a valid example of how these buildings have that special power to capture the imagination.

The enchanting Castell Coch rises in a clearing in the forest.

WELSH LIFE & CULTURE

St Fagans: National History Museum, Cardiff

Standing in the grounds of St Fagans Castle on the outskirts of Cardiff, the National History Museum is the Wales of bygone times in microcosm, a convincing exercise in time travel where visitors can take a walk through hundreds of years of Welsh life.

Over the last half-century or so, the museum has assembled a collection of more than 40 historic buildings rescued from all corners of Wales, carefully re-erecting them brick-by-brick, timber-by-timber, in beautiful 100-acre (40-hectare) parklands. The span of history is impressive, from circular Iron Age houses to dwellings from the industrial era.

Country dancing is a way of life for all ages in Wales.

Everyone who visits St Fagans has their favourites. For some it is Wales's smallest post office. Others love the village bakery, the shop, the farmsteads, tollhouse, chapel, workmen's institute or Victorian schoolhouse.

❀ National costume ❀

The national costume worn by Welsh girls on St David's Day takes its inspiration from the dress of rural women in 18th-century Wales. Its most recognisable feature is the tall black hat, but the costume also includes other traditional items such as the shawl, petticoat and apron. There is no single national costume for men.

A blacksmith at work in the 18th-century forge.

Stryd Lydan traditional barn, originally from Penley, in Flintshire.

The bakehouse – Turog is reputedly 'the most amazing bread ever'.

A particular highlight is the terrace of six ironworkers' cottages from Rhyd-y-Car, Merthyr Tydfil, which give a revealing insight into the changing lives of Wales's industrial population. Spanning the years 1805 to 1985, each house has been restored to reflect a different time period, allowing visitors to see in just a few minutes how lifestyles changed over two centuries.

Another iconic building is St Teilo's Church. Founded around 1100 at Pontarddulais near Swansea and transplanted to St Fagans, it has been painstakingly restored to its 16th-century glory with bright, colourful murals, wall paintings and carvings.

The buildings are only part of the story. The museum keeps history alive in a hands-on way with demonstrations of traditional skills and crafts. A blacksmith works in the 18th-century smithy, making horseshoes and repairing household implements. A saddler's workshop, dating from 1926, produces harnesses, collars and saddles. Traditional shawls are made at a woollen mill originally built in 1760. Visitors can also watch frequent agricultural displays and tuck in to bread and cakes made at the Derwen Bake House.

Dating from the 16th century, the Elizabethan manor house of St Fagans Castle is one of the finest structures of its kind in Wales. Its interior illustrates the castle's history at different periods of time, while also housing items from some of the country's other historic buildings. Extensive gardens in the castle grounds range from the utilitarian to the ornamental. They include an early 20th-century Italian garden, mulberry grove and rose garden, also fishponds and a vinery, and the cottage gardens where the castle's workers would grow their food. Each provides a different perspective on the lives of St Fagans' former inhabitants.

Although essentially an open-air museum, St Fagans also has the more conventional museum-style galleries and exhibition spaces displaying costumes and items from everyday life in bygone times. Most fascinating is the Oriel 1 gallery, which uses high-tech interactive exhibits to explore Welsh identity. The 1,500-year history of the Welsh language is recounted through digital stories, and visitors can learn about its links with Bengali and its place in the family of Indo-European languages. Interactive photo albums place the museum's historic buildings in context, with oral histories vividly recounting what it was like to live in them before they became museum pieces.

❀ Welsh lovespoons ❀

Dating back to the 17th century, intricately carved wooden lovespoons have traditionally been offered as a romantic gift and symbol of betrothal. They were intended to demonstrate that a potential suitor was capable of providing for his family, both through the spoon's association with food and the practical skills required to carve it. The oldest lovespoon in Wales, dating from 1667, can be seen at the Museum of Welsh Life at St Fagans.

An art, a craft and a symbolic gift.

Big Pit: National Coal Museum, Blaenavon

It is impossible to underestimate coal's impact on South Wales in landscape and human terms. At its peak in the 1920s, the coal industry employed over a quarter of a million people and there were 66 pits in the Rhondda Valleys alone. In 1913, just before the outbreak of the First World War, the country produced 56.8 million tonnes and Cardiff was the world's largest coal-exporting port.

Apart from a few small operations, coal mining in Wales has all but died out. But it is not forgotten. The National Coal Museum provides an immersive experience of this most important of Welsh industries. The 'museum' is, in effect, an authentic coalmine that looks as though the colliers have just clocked off for the day. A working pit between 1860 and 1980, the Blaenavon operation employed almost 1,400 men at its peak in 1923. Many of the mine's original

A miner at work underground in Blaencuffin coal mine, near Llanhilleth. The mine closed in 2001.

features are still here, bringing the story of the Welsh coal industry to a new generation.

Central to the Big Pit experience is the underground tour. Before descending, visitors are kitted out with hard hats, lamps and batteries, along with a 'self-rescuer' re-breather to be used in the event of an emergency. Properly attired, the pit cage carries them almost 300 feet (90 metres) down the mineshaft. Once in the pit's depths, a former miner leads an underground tour that takes in features such as the coalface, and the stables where pit ponies spent their entire working lives in darkness.

The miner's safety lamp is demonstrated on an underground tour.

Blaenavon's coal distribution flourished in the age of the steam railway.

A coal wagon in the colliery museum.

Blaenavon Ironworks stands at rest, a testament to years of hard work.

This tour never fails to impress: there is no more effective way to understand the conditions faced by Wales's miners, and the way that these shared hardships created strong community bonds both underground and back on the surface in the mining villages. As fascinating as the tour is, many will welcome the ascent back towards daylight.

The journey continues back on the surface, where a range of historic buildings builds up a complete picture of how a coalmine worked. At the winding engine-house, visitors can view in operation the massive machine that raises and lowers the mine cages. Big Pit's blacksmith can still be seen at work in the yard, while elsewhere there is the powder magazine where the pit's explosives were stored and the fan house which provided ventilation for the mine.

The pithead baths are another revelation, not just as an insight into the final part of the working day of the miner but also because of the vivid exhibitions covering a number of themes. Displays of clothing and equipment show how much the job changed over the last century and a half. The social history of the industry is also explored, addressing such topics as the children who worked in the mines, the rise of the labour movement, home life and health.

Big Pit played a major part in Blaenavon achieving World Heritage Site status, but it was not because of coal alone. The town is unusual in having a pioneering ironworks too, and evidence of the past can still be seen in the ghostly tramways and detritus of industry scattered across the mountainsides. In that sense it was a complete industrial community, a role that is further explained in the town's Heritage Centre.

The furnaces were the hub of the Blaenavon mining site.

The slate workshop.

The imposing stone and slate-dressed entrance to the National Slate Museum.

National Slate Museum, Llanberis

Slate was to North Wales what coal was to the south. It had been quarried for use in roofing as far back as Roman times, but with the advent of the Industrial Revolution it became one of Wales's most significant exports. At the industry's peak in the late 1800s, Wales was producing almost 500,000 tonnes of slate every year, most of it coming from quarries in the rugged, mountainous north-west of the country. By 1882, 92 per cent of the United Kingdom's slate originated in Wales.

During slate's heyday, Dinorwig Quarry at Llanberis was one of the biggest in Wales. It employed more than 3,000 men and, along with the quarry at nearby Penrhyn, was producing half of the country's slate. Dinorwig closed in 1969, but it has been reborn as the home of the National Slate Museum, bringing this vital piece of industrial heritage back to life.

Based around the quarry's Victorian workshops, the museum has been designed as if work has ceased only temporarily. Like Big Pit in South Wales, it is almost as if the workers have just downed tools and gone home. A wealth of preserved buildings and machines capture vividly the industry's day-to-day realities. Visitors can explore the workshops, forges and foundries arranged around the central courtyard and watch the workings of the huge waterwheel – the largest in mainland Britain – that provided their power. A painstakingly restored steam engine, so important to the industry's development, can be seen in the Loco Shed. Known as *Una*, the engine spent her working life at Penyrorsedd Quarry in Snowdonia's Nantlle Valley, before being returned to her former glory.

The home life of the quarry's former workers is also recalled. The Engineer's House has been restored to its condition of 1911. Though it is modest by today's standards, it is a step up from the row of small cottages where the ordinary quarrymen made their homes.

The Fron Haul cottages, transplanted to the museum from Tanygrisiau near Blaenau Ffestiniog, take visitors on a time trip through different eras in the lives of the quarrymen and their families. Each house has been restored to reflect a different period in the industry's history, from slate's 'Golden Age' in the late 1800s to Dinorwig's closure a century later. Perhaps the most interesting house is the one depicting the poverty-stricken life of a striking quarryman and his family during the industrial action that gripped Penrhyn Quarry at the turn of the 20th century. One of the longest-running disputes in British industrial history, the strike saw 2,800 men walk out due to disagreements over pay. The strike lasted three years, from 1900 to 1903, with around 1,000 of the strikers never returning to their jobs.

The slate industry is also kept alive here through a range of live demonstrations. Visitors can witness skills built up through generations of working with slate. The surprisingly delicate art of splitting slate to wafer-thin slices can be seen, but the craftsmen are also past masters at even more intricate work, carving everything from picture frames to fans out of the dark stone. The work of the blacksmiths, carpenters and mechanics that kept the quarry functioning smoothly is also showcased in daily presentations.

When you visit North Wales you will inevitably see evidence of the historic slate industry in abandoned quarries carved into the hillsides. The National Slate Museum brings meaning and context to these ghostly sites.

Slates loaded on a wagon, prior to being transported from the site.

Penrhyn Slate Quarry in 1852, an awe-inspiring setting.

National Waterfront Museum, Swansea

South Wales was changed beyond all recognition by the Industrial Revolution. As a major producer of coal, steel and tin, the region underwent a social and technological revolution. The National Waterfront Museum, in Swansea's Maritime Quarter, celebrates and explains this extraordinary period in Welsh history.

Heavy industry brought rapid evolution to a country where travelling by horseback had previously been the fastest way of getting around. Cargoes of coal and steel had to be moved quickly from production centres to the growing cities and to ports, for export across the world. The museum houses many examples of the transportation and industrial innovations of the last 300 years, including a replica of the very first steam train to run on rails. The machine, built by Richard Trevithick at Pen-y-Darren Ironworks in Merthyr Tydfil in 1804, predates George

The giant-sized cog and gears of the brick press.

Stephenson's more famous *Rocket* by more than two decades. The museum also includes exhibits such as a massive water-powered tilt hammer used for shaping wrought iron, and a tinplate rolling mill.

In addition, the museum tells the human story. Industry's huge impact on Welsh society is recalled in the 'People, Communities and Lives' exhibition. Clever, contemporary interactive technology is used to involve the visitor in this historic tale,

The highly impressive replica steam locomotive.

❊ A Welsh revolution ❊

The Industrial Revolution's impact on Wales was seismic, radically reshaping the country in ways that remain visible to this day. At the beginning of the 19th century Wales was an overwhelmingly rural nation, with the large majority of its population making a living off the land. By 1851, however, two-thirds of Welsh families were supported by non-agricultural activities.

Mines and foundries producing coal, slate, tin, copper, iron and steel sprung up, mainly in the south-east and north-west. Merthyr Tydfil in South Wales, for example, rapidly changed from a sleepy settlement to the bustling 'iron capital of the world'. The Valleys of South Wales were transformed by hundreds of coalmines and the terraced communities that grew up around them. In North Wales, slate mining had a similar impact.

The period also saw a revolution in transportation as canals, roads, railways and docks were built to facilitate the movement of Wales's industrial bounty.

providing hands-on insights into the country's changing social fabric. A timeline reflecting Swansea's status as a hub of Wales's maritime industry tracks the nation's long relationship with the sea. Politics also come into play when the museum reflects on how an increasingly industrialized workforce gave rise to organizations like the trade unions and Miners' Association.

State-of-the-art: the National Waterfront Museum, Swansea.

Historic boats moored at the Maritime Quarter, Swansea.

National Museum, Cardiff

Taking pride of place in Cardiff's neo-classical civic centre, the National Museum houses an eclectic collection embracing art, archaeology, geology and natural history. Along with its permanent collections, it also plays host to major touring and temporary exhibitions.

Of all its treasures, art is possibly the most glittering. The museum is home to the National Museum of Art. Opened in July 2011, it brings Wales's entire collection together in a series of integrated galleries, divided into Contemporary, Impressionist and Modern, Historic and Applied art. As well as showcasing art from Wales, the museum holds an impressive range of pieces from around the world.

Of particular note is the extensive collection – one of the largest in Britain – of impressionist and post-impressionist paintings, with works from artists such as Claude Monet, Vincent Van Gogh and Pierre-Auguste Renoir. Welsh art is well represented too, with galleries containing pieces from 1550 to the present day. These include portraits from the Tudor period, 18th-century paintings inspired by druidic traditions and works from 20th-century Welsh artists like Augustus and Gwen John.

An aerial view of the museum's classical-style interior.

The wide-ranging natural history gallery examines the diverse range of habitats found in Wales, from sea and coastline to mountain and woodland. Amid the seabirds of Skomer Island and displays of plant life, a trio of sea creatures make up perhaps the most striking exhibits. The huge basking shark and 30-foot (9-metre) humpback whale skeleton are genuinely awe-inspiring, but pick of the crop is the giant leatherback turtle. Washed up on the shore near Harlech Castle in 1988, this almost 10 foot (3-metre) long, 2,000lb (907 kilogram) monster is the largest specimen of its type ever recorded.

An ancient Celtic cross on display in Cardiff's National Museum.

Rodin's famous bronze The Kiss, *in the National Museum.*

The Evolution of Wales gallery employs a combination of spectacular audio-visual technology and exhibits to take visitors through 4.6 billion years of Welsh history. Starting with the Big Bang, the exhibition shows how the piece of land that would eventually become Wales began its life below the equator, before undertaking an incredible journey to the northern hemisphere. Along the way it has provided a habitat for an astonishing menagerie of creatures, from dinosaurs to woolly mammoths, many of which are represented here in dramatically staged tableaux. The gallery also explains the slow geological processes that created the coal deposits which played such a crucial role in Wales's Industrial Revolution.

The history of the country's people is traced in Origins: In Search of Early Wales. Starting with the earliest known humans 230,000 years ago, the exhibition shows man's development through to the medieval period. Packed with rare archaeological finds, each backed up with information placing them in context, Origins shines a light on the changing lives of Wales's historic inhabitants. Also on display are the beautiful Capel Isaf Armlets, some of the earliest gold objects found in Wales, as well as artefacts from both the Roman and Viking invasions of the country.

A prize-winning visual art installation by Wu Chi-Tsung.

A close encounter with a fearsome model dinosaur.

Houses & Gardens

Wales has a wealth of outstanding historic homes and gardens throughout the length and breadth of the country. These are just a small selection.

Llanerchaeron near Aberaeron, is a rare example of a self-sufficient 18th-century 'gentleman's estate'. The villa, built in 1795 by celebrated architect John Nash, is surrounded by extensive outbuildings that reveal the workings of a Welsh country estate of that era.

Eighty-acre (30-hectare) **Bodnant Garden** near Conwy is a constantly changing palette of colour. Early spring sees outstanding blooms of daffodils, magnolias and camellias, while the 180-foot (54-metre) long laburnum arch – possibly Bodnant's most celebrated feature – bursts into flower during May.

Penrhyn Castle near Bangor is a dramatic 'sham' castle built by a wealthy 19th-century industrialist. Its vast interior, impressive collection of art, one-tonne slate bed made for Queen Victoria and lavish staterooms are an unashamed statement of wealth and power. The castle's 60-acre (24-hectare) grounds contain an exotic tree collection and Victorian walled garden.

The Great Glasshouse at the National Botanic Garden.

The vast **National Botanic Garden of Wales** in Carmarthenshire is both a visitor attraction and conservation centre. The massive dome of the Great Glasshouse, its iconic feature, provides a climate-controlled environment for rare plants from several continents, while many other magnificent specimens can be seen in the historic double-walled garden.

The garden sitting in the shadow of **Powis Castle**, near Welshpool, is world-renowned. The Italian-influenced terraces, embellished with original lead statues, distinguish it from the majority of its British peers. The castle itself houses a large collection of paintings, sculptures and tapestries, along with a fabulous treasury of Indian artefacts amassed by the Clive family in the 18th century.

Azaleas in bloom, one of many pleasures at Bodnant Garden.

CATHEDRALS, ABBEYS & CHURCHES

Although the early Celtic Church was part of the Roman Papal system, it had its own distinct personality. Little of the bureaucracy of the parent church penetrated this relatively remote location. With bishops and cathedrals in faraway cities, worshippers were more likely to take their lead from the nearby monasteries. One such place was at Henllan, now Hentland on Wye, in Herefordshire. It was here that Dyfrig, the first saint of the Celtic Church, was based in the 4th century AD.

Religious sites can be found all over Wales. Of particular interest are the holy wells, the most

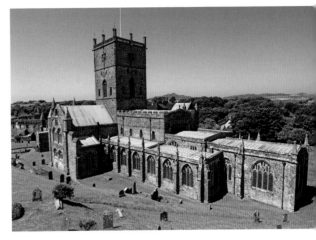

Magnificent St Davids Cathedral, in Pembrokeshire, is Wales's national church.

Tintern Abbey, in Gwent, a haven of peace and quiet.

Capel y Ffin chapel, in the Vale of Ewyas, Black Mountains.

famous of which is aptly named **Holywell**, near Flint. Many predated the arrival of Christianity, and early missionaries would often build churches at these sites in an effort to stamp out the native religions.

Wales's iconic religious site is the spectacular purple-stoned **St Davids Cathedral**, in the far west of Pembrokeshire. Founded by Wales's patron saint, a church has stood on the site since the 6th century. It remains a spiritually charged place of worship and pilgrimage to the present day.

Ruined medieval abbeys like **Tintern** and **Valle Crucis**, Llangollen, also retain the power to evoke awe and contemplation.

Chapels are another major feature of Wales's religious landscape. They sprang up across the country in the early 1900s, as Welsh Nonconformists sought to distance themselves from the Church of England. Although the chapels themselves are visually unassuming, it was within their walls that the choir-singing now synonymous with Wales was nurtured.

A SPORTING NATION

It is impossible to mention sport in Wales without immediately thinking of rugby. Since the first Welsh international team was fielded in 1881, the game has been a national obsession. The Welsh sides of the 1930s and 1970s dominated the game and, with the triumphant wins in the 2012 Grand Slam and 2013 Six Nations tournaments, enthusiasm for rugby remains undimmed. Match days in Cardiff transform the city into a sea of red as tens of thousands of fans flock to the Millennium Stadium, built for Wales's hosting of the Rugby World Cup in 1999.

Wales is also home to some less familiar and more unusual sporting events. Each summer, the little town of Llanwrtyd Wells holds the Man versus Horse Marathon. Following an overheard conversation in the local pub about whether a man could outpace a horse in a cross-country race, the first event was organized in 1980 by landlord Gordon Green. Unsurprisingly, horses have tended to come out on top, though human competitors managed to snatch victory in 2004 and 2007. Llanwrtyd also hosts other strange events, including the truly unique International Bog Snorkelling Championships.

Rugby: the national sport and passion.

Inspired by the exploits of Welsh runner Guto Nyth Brân, the Nos Galan Races take place every New Year's Eve in Mountain Ash in the Welsh Valleys. Born in 1700, Guto was reputedly so fast he could catch a bird in flight and once made a seven-mile (11-km) round trip to shop in Pontypridd before his mother could boil the breakfast kettle. Entrants in the 3-mile (5-km) race are traditionally joined by a mystery sportsman, whose identity is only revealed on the day of the event.

The man – or woman – versus horse race, a test of stamina and fortitude for both.

A TASTE OF WALES

One of the most instantly recognisable traditional Welsh foods is laverbread. Made from the *Porphyra umbilicalis* seaweed common to Britain's western shores, it has been a part of the local diet for centuries. Rich in iron and vitamins, laverbread is typically eaten as a breakfast dish served with bacon and possibly cockles, another Welsh delicacy. The little molluscs have been harvested at Penclawdd on the Gower Peninsula since Roman times. Cockles remain a popular seller at the markets of Swansea and Cardiff, served simply with a little white pepper and vinegar.

The warming, hearty broth known as *cawl* is another favourite with a long lineage. Commonly served during the cold winter months and made with whatever seasonal produce was available, there is no single definitive recipe for the dish. Today it often features the Welsh staples of lamb and leek, but the exact ingredients vary from kitchen to kitchen.

However, you would be wrong to imagine that Wales's food culture is stuck in the past. Recent years have seen a culinary revolution focused on the innovative use of fresh local produce from land and sea, to satisfy contemporary tastes.

Cockles and laverbread, a tasty combination.

Highly regarded regional fare such as Welsh Black beef, salt marsh lamb and a wide range of artisan farmhouses cheeses are putting a new spin on the Welsh food tradition.

Farmers' markets catering to the growing interest in authentic Welsh produce and the importance of provenance in food are held across the country, while annual events such as Abergavenny Food Festival – one of the UK's top foodie gatherings – provide a showcase for the many delicacies that Wales has to offer.

A plate of traditional mouth-watering Welsh cakes, cooked on a griddle, are irresistible.

PLACES TO VISIT

Castles & Historic Sites

Beaumaris Castle, Isle of Anglesey LL85 8AP (CADW)
www.beaumaris.com

Caernarfon Castle, Caernarfon, Gwynedd LL55 2AY (CADW)
www.cadw.wales.gov.uk

Caerphilly Castle, Caerphilly CF83 1JD (CADW)
www.cadw.wales.gov.uk

Cardiff Castle, Cardiff CF10 3RB
www.cardiffcastle.com

Carreg Cennen Castle, Llandeilo, Carmarthenshire SA19 6UA (CADW)
www.cadw.wales.gov.uk

Castell Coch, Tongwynlais, Cardiff CF15 7JS (CADW)
www.cadw.wales.gov.uk

Castell Henllys, Panglas Velindre, Crymych, Dyfed SA41 3UT
www.castellhenllys.com
A reconstructed Iron Age fort with three reconstructed roundhouses, a granary and a forge, the site dates back to c. 400 BC; located just off the A487 main coastal road between Newport and Cardigan in north Pembrokeshire.

Chepstow Castle, Chepstow, Monmouthshire NP16 5EY (CADW)
www.cadw.wales.gov.uk

Iron Age hut, Castell Henllys.

Conwy Castle, Conwy LL32 8AY (CADW)
www.cadw.wales.gov.uk

Harlech Castle, Harlech, Gwynedd LL46 2YH (CADW)
www.cadw.wales.gov.uk

Pembroke Castle, Pembroke, Pembrokeshire SA71 4LA
www.pembroke-castle.co.uk

Museums & Industrial Sites

Big Pit: National Coal Museum, Blaenavon, Torfaen NP4 9XP
www.museumwales.ac.uk/bigpit

National Museum Cardiff, Cathays Park, Cardiff CF10 3NP
www.museumwales.ac.uk/cardiff

National Slate Museum, Llanberis, Gwynedd LL55 4TY
www.museumwales.ac.uk/slate

Llechwedd Slate Caverns, Blaenau Ffestiniog, Gwynedd LL41 3NB
www.llechwedd-slate-caverns.co.uk
Journey nearly half a mile into the mine, descending deep underground on a cable railway, to see ten vast caverns and a subterranean lake.

National Waterfront Museum, Swansea SA1 3RD
www.museumwales.ac.uk/en.swansea

National Wool Museum, Dre-Fach Felindre, Llandysul, Carmarthenshire SA44 5UP
www.museumwales.ac.uk/wool

Rhondda Heritage Park, Pontypridd, Mid Glamorgan CF37 2NP
www.rhonddaheritagepark.com
Based at a former colliery, the park displays life in the Welsh valleys and visitors can tour a working coalmine and a period village street.

St Fagans: National History Museum, St Fagans, Cardiff CF5 6XB
www.museumwales.ac.uk/stfagans